INSIDE THE NBA

LOS ANGELES LAKERS

Sam Moussavi and
Samantha Nugent

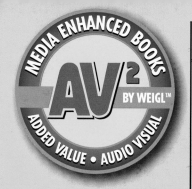

AV² provides enriched content that supplements and complements this book. Weigl's AV² books strive to create inspired learning and engage young minds in a total learning experience.

Go to www.av2books.com, and enter this book's unique code.

BOOK CODE

W 5 4 3 2 3 3

AV² by Weigl brings you media enhanced books that support active learning.

Your AV² Media Enhanced books come alive with...

Audio
Listen to sections of the book read aloud.

Video
Watch informative video clips.

Embedded Weblinks
Gain additional information for research.

Try This!
Complete activities and hands-on experiments.

Key Words
Study vocabulary, and complete a matching word activity.

Quizzes
Test your knowledge.

Slide Show
View images and captions, and prepare a presentation.

... and much, much more!

Published by AV² by Weigl
350 5th Avenue, 59th Floor
New York, NY 10118
Website: www.av2books.com

Library of Congress Control Number: 2016935105

ISBN: 978-1-4896-4697-2 (Hardcover)
ISBN: 978-1-4896-4698-9 (Multi-user eBook)

Printed in the United States of America in Brainerd, Minnesota
1 2 3 4 5 6 7 8 9 0   20 19 18 17 16

082016
200516

Project Coordinator Heather Kissock
Art Director Terry Paulhus

Photo Credits
Every reasonable effort has been made to trace ownership and to obtain permission to reprint copyright material. The publishers would be pleased to have any errors or omissions brought to their attention so that they may be corrected in subsequent printings.

Weigl acknowledges Newscom, Getty Images, and Alamy as its primary image suppliers for this title.

LOS ANGELES LAKERS

CONTENTS

Introduction

The Los Angeles Lakers **franchise** is one of the most successful franchises in National Basketball Association (NBA) history. The Lakers have won 16 NBA Titles, second only to the 17 titles held by the Boston Celtics. From the time the team was created in Minneapolis to its move to Los Angeles, the Lakers franchise has relied on superstar players to lead the way to championships.

The star players on the court fit in perfectly with the celebrities in the city of Los Angeles. The teams of the 1980s, led by Earvin "Magic" Johnson and Kareem Abdul-Jabbar, were some of the most popular in franchise history. Los Angeles experienced a relatively down period in the 1990s, with no NBA Titles.

Drafted in 2014, forward Julius Randle puts up an average of 11.6 points per game for the Lakers.

The Lakers teams of the 2000s added to the franchise's championship count, this time on the shoulders of stars Shaquille O'Neal and Kobe Bryant. Today, the Lakers face the new challenge of trying to rebuild after many years of success and many superstar players. They will need to regroup in order to make it through the **playoffs** once again.

LOS ANGELES LAKERS

Arena Staples Center

Division Pacific Division (Western **Conference**)

Head Coach Luke Walton

Location Los Angeles, California

NBA Championships 16

Nickname(s) Lake Show

9 Retired Numbers

23 Division Titles

31 Conference Titles

60 Playoff Appearances

68 NBA Seasons

Point guard and shooting guard Jordan Clarkson was drafted by the Lakers in 2014.

History

$$$

Worth $2.7 billion, the Lakers are the **second-most valuable** NBA franchise.

In 2005, Lou Williams was drafted to the NBA directly out of high school. In 2015, he was traded to the Lakers and put up 21 points for them in his very first game.

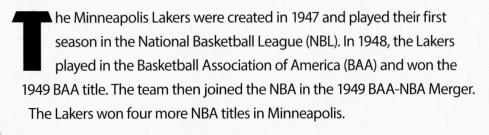

The Minneapolis Lakers were created in 1947 and played their first season in the National Basketball League (NBL). In 1948, the Lakers played in the Basketball Association of America (BAA) and won the 1949 BAA title. The team then joined the NBA in the 1949 BAA-NBA Merger. The Lakers won four more NBA titles in Minneapolis.

Before the 1960–61 season, the franchise moved to southern California and became the Los Angeles Lakers. Superstars Elgin Baylor, Jerry West, and Wilt Chamberlain played for the team during those early years in Los Angeles. In 1972, the Lakers won their first NBA title in Los Angeles. Perhaps the greatest period in Lakers history came in the 1980s when the team was led by coach Pat Riley, Kareem Abdul-Jabbar, and Magic Johnson.

The teams of the 1980s were called the "Showtime" Lakers because of the way they pushed the ball up the floor on offense. This entertaining style helped the Lakers win five NBA titles from 1980 to 1988. After struggling in the 1990s, the team regained its form in 2000, behind coach Phil Jackson, and players Shaquille O'Neal and Kobe Bryant. Los Angeles won three straight NBA Championships from 2000 to 2002, and then two more in 2009 and 2010.

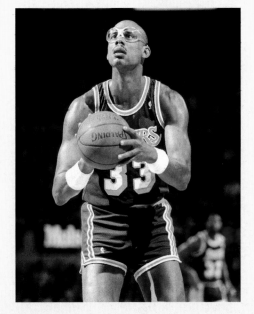

Center Kareem Abdul-Jabbar was traded to the Lakers in 1975 and played with the team for 14 years.

The Arena

There are more than **1,200** television monitors throughout Staples Center.

Staples Center is the only arena shared by two NBA teams. It is the home arena of both the Los Angeles Clippers and the Los Angeles Lakers.

The Minneapolis Lakers played at the Minneapolis Auditorium from 1947 to 1959. The team played at the Minneapolis Auditorium while it was part of the NBL, BAA, and NBA. The Lakers won five championships while in this arena. During the Lakers' last season in Minneapolis, the team played at the Minneapolis Armory.

In Los Angeles, the Lakers first played at the Los Angeles Memorial Sports Arena. The Lakers played at Memorial Sports Arena from 1960 to 1967. The team then moved to the Forum, which was renamed Great Western Forum, in nearby Inglewood, California. The Lakers played at the Forum from 1967 to 1999. The arena was home to the team during the popular "Showtime" era. The Lakers won six NBA titles while at the Forum.

Before the 1999–2000 season, the Lakers moved into Staples Center, a brand new arena located in downtown Los Angeles. The team won three NBA titles during its first three seasons playing at Staples Center in 2000, 2001, and 2002. The Lakers have won a total of five NBA Championships while playing at Staples Center.

During the year, Staples Center floor is changed many times depending on which team, or sport, is playing at home next.

Where They Play

British Columbia
Alberta
Saskatchewan
Manitoba
Ontario

Washington
Montana
North Dakota
Minnesota **7**
Wisconsin **25**

9
Oregon
Idaho
South Dakota
Iowa **21**
Illinois

5
Nevada
Wyoming
Nebraska

1
Utah **10**
Colorado
Kansas
Missouri

California
2
6

3
Staples Center, Los Angeles
Arizona
New Mexico
Oklahoma **8**
Arkansas **13**

4
11
Mis

Pacific Ocean
Texas
Louisiana

15
12 *Gulf of Mexico*

Inside the NBA

PACIFIC DIVISION
1. Golden State Warriors
2. Los Angeles Clippers
★ 3. Los Angeles Lakers
4. Phoenix Suns
5. Sacramento Kings

NORTHWEST DIVISION
6. Denver Nuggets
7. Minnesota Timberwolves
8. Oklahoma City Thunder
9. Portland Trail Blazers
10. Utah Jazz

SOUTHWEST DIVISION
11. Dallas Mavericks
12. Houston Rockets
13. Memphis Grizzlies
14. New Orleans Pelicans
15. San Antonio Spurs

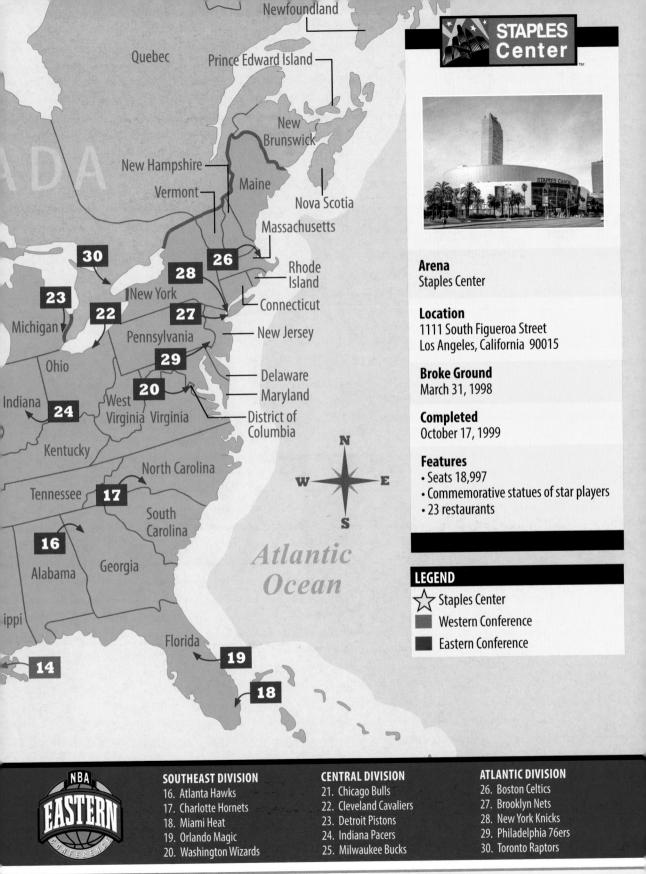

Newfoundland

Quebec

Prince Edward Island

New Brunswick

New Hampshire

Maine

Vermont

Nova Scotia

Massachusetts

Rhode Island

Connecticut

New York

New Jersey

Michigan

Pennsylvania

Ohio

Delaware

Maryland

Indiana

West Virginia   Virginia

District of Columbia

Kentucky

North Carolina

Tennessee

South Carolina

Alabama   Georgia

Atlantic Ocean

Florida

30   23   22   28   26   27   29   20   24   17   16   14   19   18

N
W   E
S

STAPLES Center

Arena
Staples Center

Location
1111 South Figueroa Street
Los Angeles, California 90015

Broke Ground
March 31, 1998

Completed
October 17, 1999

Features
• Seats 18,997
• Commemorative statues of star players
• 23 restaurants

LEGEND
☆ Staples Center
▇ Western Conference
▇ Eastern Conference

NBA EASTERN CONFERENCE

SOUTHEAST DIVISION
16. Atlanta Hawks
17. Charlotte Hornets
18. Miami Heat
19. Orlando Magic
20. Washington Wizards

CENTRAL DIVISION
21. Chicago Bulls
22. Cleveland Cavaliers
23. Detroit Pistons
24. Indiana Pacers
25. Milwaukee Bucks

ATLANTIC DIVISION
26. Boston Celtics
27. Brooklyn Nets
28. New York Knicks
29. Philadelphia 76ers
30. Toronto Raptors

The Uniforms

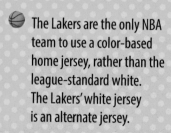

12 The Lakers played **12** games in their alternate white uniforms during the 2015–16 season.

The Lakers are the only NBA team to use a color-based home jersey, rather than the league-standard white. The Lakers' white jersey is an alternate jersey.

I n Minneapolis, the Lakers' colors were powder blue and gold. The home uniform was white with powder blue and gold trim, and the away uniform was powder blue with gold trim. Both uniforms read "MPLS," the abbreviation for Minneapolis, across the chest.

HOME

AWAY

When the team moved to Los Angeles in 1960, it changed its colors to royal blue, powder blue, and white. The home uniform was white with royal blue and powder blue trim. The away uniform was royal blue with powder blue and white trim. Both uniforms read "Los Angeles" across the chest.

In 1967, the franchise changed its colors to purple and gold. Today, the Lakers use this same color scheme. The home uniform is gold with purple and white trim. The away uniform is purple with gold and white trim. Both uniforms read "Lakers" across the chest.

While the Lakers' purple away jerseys have changed little, their gold home jerseys have seen several changes. Changes have been made to the font, lettering, and trim.

The Coaches

The Lakers won **67** games during Phil Jackson's first season as coach in 1999–2000.

Luke Walton won two NBA championships while playing for the Lakers.

The Los Angeles Lakers have had 26 head coaches during their 68 seasons in the NBA. Many of those coaches have led the Lakers to the NBA postseason. Several coaches, including Phil Jackson and Pat Riley, have won NBA titles with the franchise. Former Lakers star players Magic Johnson, Jerry West, and George Mikan have coached the team as well.

PAT RILEY Pat Riley took over as coach of the Los Angeles Lakers early in the 1981–82 season. Riley was coach of the team during the its "Showtime" era and won four NBA championships in 1982, 1985, 1987, and 1988. He is second on the list of coaches with the most regular season wins, with 533.

PHIL JACKSON Phil Jackson became head coach of the Los Angeles Lakers before the 1999–2000 season. Before that, Jackson was the coach of the Chicago Bulls and won six NBA titles with the team. With the Lakers, he won five NBA titles in 11 seasons. Jackson is first on the Lakers' coaching wins list, with 610 regular season wins.

LUKE WALTON Luke Walton was hired as the Los Angeles Lakers head coach on April 29, 2016. Walton was an assistant coach with the Golden State Warriors for two seasons before joining the Lakers. He played with the Los Angeles Lakers for nine seasons, from 2003 to 2012.

Team Spirit

Former Lakers owner Jerry Buss created the Laker Girls in 1979 to add more entertainment to the arena experience.

The Los Angeles Lakers are one of four NBA franchises that do not have a mascot. In fact, the franchise has never had a mascot. Instead, the team has a cheerleading squad called the Laker Girls. The Laker Girls perform dance routines during every Lakers home game. The squad was created before the 1979–80 season, when the Lakers played at the Forum.

The Laker Girls perform 30 different dance routines over the course of a season. Each member must audition to make the squad, and each returning member must audition to keep her spot from the season before. Each season, the Laker Girls help at about 25 charity events held around the Los Angeles area.

fun facts

#1 Well-known singer Paula Abdul was a member of the Laker Girls before her entertainment career began.

#2 The Laker Girls performed in China during a fan appreciation day event in 2013.

Superstars

Many great players have suited up for the Lakers. A few of them have become icons of the team and the city it represents.

Elgin Baylor

The Minneapolis Lakers selected Elgin Baylor with the first overall pick in the 1958 **NBA Draft**. Baylor emerged as a scoring threat, winning the 1959 NBA Rookie of the Year Award. He played his entire 14-season career with the Lakers franchise. Baylor played in 11 **All-Star** games and was a member of the Lakers' 1972 NBA title team. He finished his career with averages of 27 points and 13 **rebounds** per game. Baylor was inducted into the Basketball Hall of Fame in 1977.

Position: Forward
NBA Seasons: 14 (1958–1972)
Born: September 16, 1934, Washington, D.C., United States

Kareem Abdul-Jabbar

The Milwaukee Bucks traded center Kareem Abdul-Jabbar to the Los Angeles Lakers before the 1975–76 season. Abdul-Jabbar played 14 seasons in Los Angeles, from 1975 to 1989. He won five NBA championships with the Lakers in 1980, 1982, 1985, 1987, and 1988. With the Lakers, Abdul-Jabbar made 13 All-Star teams and won the NBA MVP Award three times in 1976, 1977, and 1980. He finished his Lakers career with averages of 22 points, 9 rebounds, 3 **assists**, and 2 **blocks**. Abdul-Jabbar was inducted to the Basketball Hall of Fame in 1995.

Position: Center
NBA Seasons: 20 (1969–1989)
Born: April 16, 1947, New York City, New York, United States

Shaquille O'Neal

Shaquille O'Neal joined the Los Angeles Lakers as a **free agent** before the 1996–97 season. Before moving west, O'Neal played for the Orlando Magic, from 1992 to 1996. He played eight seasons for the Lakers ,from 1996 to 2004, and won thee NBA titles in 2000, 2001, and 2002. O'Neal won the NBA MVP Award in 2000 and made seven All-Star appearances. He held Lakers career averages of 25 points, 11 rebounds, 3 assists, and 2 blocks. O'Neal was inducted into the Basketball Hall of Fame in 2014. He had one of the most dominating inside games and was known for his ferocious slam dunks.

Position: Center
NBA Seasons: 19 (1992–2011)
Born: March 6, 1972, Newark, New Jersey, United States

Kobe Bryant

The Los Angeles Lakers traded for Kobe Bryant on draft night in 1996. Bryant came into the NBA from Lower Merion High School in Pennsylvania. Bryant spent all of his 20 seasons in the NBA with the Lakers. He won the 2008 MVP Award along with five NBA titles. Bryant also made 18 All-Star appearances. He scored 81 points in a single game against the Toronto Raptors in 2006, the second-highest individual point total in NBA history. Bryant holds career averages of 25 points, 5 rebounds, and 4 assists per game. He retired from the NBA in 2016.

Position: Shooting Guard/Small Forward
NBA Seasons: 20 (1996–2016)
Born: August 23, 1978, Philadelphia, Pennsylvania, United States

The Greatest of All Time

There are several standout players on the Lakers roster who have worked hard to push the team to success. Often, there is one player who has become known as the "Greatest of All Time," or GOAT. This player has gone above and beyond to achieve greatness and to help his team shine.

Magic Johnson

Position: Point Guard • **NBA Seasons:** 13 (1979–1991 and 1995–96)
Born: August 14, 1959, Lansing, Michigan, United States

Earvin "Magic" Johnson was selected by the Los Angeles Lakers with the first overall pick in the 1979 NBA Draft. Johnson attended college at Michigan State University. He was nicknamed "Magic" because of the way he dished out "no-look" passes. Johnson made a name for himself in the NBA by helping the Lakers win the 1980 **NBA Finals** and taking home the Finals' MVP trophy.

Johnson won five NBA titles for the "Showtime" Lakers. He also made 12 NBA All-Star teams and 9 All-NBA First teams. Magic finished his career with averages of 19 points, 11 assists, and 7 rebounds per game. He is the Lakers franchise leader in assists and also won three NBA MVP Awards. Johnson retired from the NBA in 1996 and was inducted into the Basketball Hall of Fame in 2006.

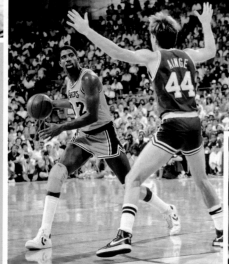

Magic Johnson is the only rookie to ever win the Finals MVP trophy.

Johnson played all 13 seasons of his NBA career with the Lakers.

fun facts

#1 During the 1988–89 season, Johnson had a .911 **free throw** average.

#2 Magic Johnson's single-season assist record is 977.

#3 He stole the ball 1,724 times in his career.

#4 In his career, Magic Johnson played a total of 33,245 minutes.

Johnson retired briefly in 1991, only to come back and play in the 1992 All-Star Game. During the game, he was awarded his second All-Star Game MVP.

The Moment

Kareem Abdul-Jabbar was the league MVP during the 1979–1980 season. Even though he did not play in game 6 of the finals, he still hoisted the championship trophy after the Lakers' win.

The greatest moment in Lakers history came during game 6 of the 1980 NBA Finals. The Lakers were going up against the Philadelphia 76ers. The Lakers won 60 games during the 1979–80 season and were led by rookie Magic Johnson and Kareem Abdul-Jabbar.

The two teams split the first four games of the series, and in every game the score was close. The series went back to Los Angeles for game 5, where the Lakers won in another close match. Unfortunately, in game 5, Abdul-Jabbar hurt his ankle, putting his ability to play in game 6 in doubt.

Game 6 in Philadelphia saw Abdul-Jabbar sidelined. The Lakers inserted Johnson, who was a point guard, into Abdul-Jabbar's starting center position. Johnson posted 42 points, 15 rebounds, and 7 assists. The Lakers crushed the 76ers and won the 1980 NBA Finals. Fans still talk about Magic Johnson's brilliance on that night.

Throughout game 6 of the 1980 Finals, Magic Johnson played all five positions at some point during the game.

Although Abdul-Jabbar missed one game of the series, he was still the highest scorer for the Lakers during the 1980 Finals, with 167 points.

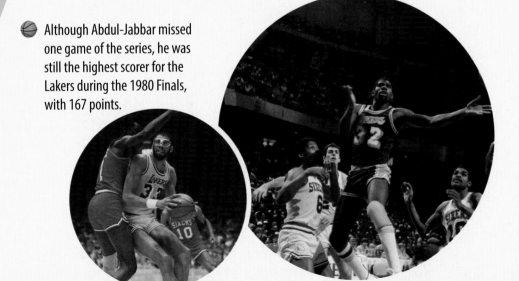

All-Time Records

393

Most Three Pointers Made in Season

183 In 1994–95, Los Angeles Lakers point guard Nick Van Exel set the **single-season record** for most three pointers made, with 183.

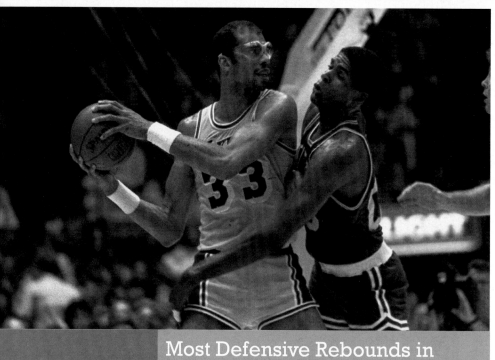

Most Defensive Rebounds in a Season

1,111 Lakers center Kareem Abdul-Jabbar pulled down a single-season, NBA-record 1,111 rebounds during the 1975–76 season.

336

Most Blocks in a Season

Los Angeles Lakers center Elmore Smith set the single-season record for most blocks, with 393 during the 1973–74 season.

44%

Highest Three Point Field Goal Percentage in a Season

During the 2008–09 season, Lakers forward Vladimir Radmanovic made a single-season record 44 percent of his three pointers.

Most Offensive Rebounds in a Season

O'Neal set the Los Angeles Lakers' single-season record for most offensive rebounds, with 336 in 1999–00.

989

Most Assists in a Season

In 1990–91, Magic Johnson set the Lakers' single-season record for most assists, with 989.

Timeline

Throughout the team's history, the Lakers have had many memorable events that have become defining moments for the team and its fans.

1947–1949

The Minneapolis Lakers are created and play in the National Basketball League (NBL) in 1947. In 1948, the team joins the Basketball Association of America (BAA). The Lakers win the 1949 BAA Title.

1951–1954

Minneapolis wins three straight NBA titles in 1952, 1953, and 1954.

1950 **1960** **1970** **1980**

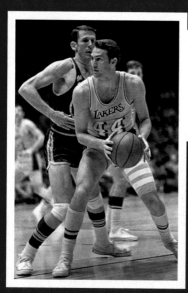

1960

The franchise moves west to southern California and are now known as the Los Angeles Lakers. The Lakers become the NBA's first West Coast team.

1979

Los Angeles select point guard Earvin "Magic" Johnson with the first overall pick in the 1979 NBA Draft. Johnson teams up with Abdul-Jabbar to form a successful duo for much of the 1980s.

1979–1988

The "Showtime" Lakers, led by coach Pat Riley, players Johnson, Abdul-Jabbar, James Worthy, and Michael Cooper win five NBA titles in the 1980s. After the 1988 Finals, the franchise wins 11 NBA Championships.

1999–2002

Led by coach Phil Jackson, Bryant, and O'Neal, the Lakers win three straight NBA titles in 2000, 2001, and 2002. Guard Derek Fisher, and forwards Robert Horry and Rick Fox, are instrumental in winning three NBA Championships in a row.

1996

After struggling for much of the early 1990s, Los Angeles signs superstar center Shaquille O'Neal as a free agent. Then, on draft night, Los Angeles trades for high school phenomenon Kobe Bryant.

2006

Bryant scores 81 points in one game against the Toronto Raptors. This is the second-highest total in NBA history, behind Wilt Chamberlain's 100 points on March 2, 1962.

1990   **2000**   **2010**   **2020**

2008–2010

Los Angeles wins two straight NBA titles in 2009 and 2010. In 2009, the Lakers defeat the Orlando Magic and in 2010, the Boston Celtics in two grueling seven-game series. The franchise has now won 16 championships.

The Future

The Lakers of today are led by coach Luke Walton. The team also has second-year forward Julius Randle and rookie guard D'Angelo Russell. Los Angeles has not made the playoffs since 2013. The team hopes to develop its young talent and reach the top of the Western Conference again.

Write a Biography

Life Story

A person's life story can be the subject of a book. This kind of book is called a biography. Biographies often describe the lives of people who have achieved great success. These people may be alive today, or they may have lived many years ago. Reading a biography can help you learn more about a great person.

Get the Facts

Use this book, and research in the library and on the internet, to find out more about your favorite star. Learn as much about this player as you can. What position does he play? What are his statistics in important categories? Has he set any records? Also, be sure to write down key events in the person's life. What was his childhood like? What has he accomplished off the court? Is there anything else that makes this person special or unusual?

Use the Concept Web

A concept web is a useful research tool. Read the questions in the concept web on the following page. Answer the questions in your notebook. Your answers will help you write a biography.

Concept Web

Your Opinion
- What did you learn from the books you read in your research?
- Would you suggest these books to others?
- Was anything missing from these books?

Adulthood
- Where does this individual currently reside?
- Does he or she have a family?

Childhood
- Where and when was this person born?
- Describe his or her parents, siblings, and friends.
- Did this person grow up in unusual circumstances?

Accomplishments off the Court
- What is this person's life's work?
- Has he or she received awards or recognition for accomplishments?
- How have this person's accomplishments served others?

Write a Biography

Help and Obstacles
- Did this individual have a positive attitude?
- Did he or she receive help from others?
- Did this person have a mentor?
- Did this person face any hardships?
- If so, how were the hardships overcome?

Accomplishments on the Court
- What records does this person hold?
- What key games and plays have defined his career?
- What are his stats in categories important to his position?

Work and Preparation
- What was this person's education?
- What was his or her work experience?
- How does this person work?
- What is the process he or she uses?

Trivia Time

Take this quiz to test your knowledge of the Los Angeles Lakers.
The answers are printed upside down under each question.

1 Which team traded Kareem Abdul-Jabbar to the Lakers?

A. Milwaukee Bucks

2 When did the Lakers franchise win its first NBA title in Los Angeles?

A. 1972

3 Where do the Lakers currently play their home games?

A. Staples Center

4 How many NBA titles did coach Phil Jackson win with the Lakers?

A. Five

5 When was Elgin Baylor inducted into the Basketball Hall of Fame?

A. 1977

6 How many seasons did Shaquille O'Neal play with the Lakers?

A. Eight

7 Which team did Kobe Bryant score 81 points in a single game against in 2006?

A. Toronto Raptors

8 How many minutes did Magic Johnson play in his career?

A. 33,245

9 When did the Lakers move from Minneapolis to Los Angeles?

A. 1960

10 Where did Magic Johnson go to college?

A. Michigan State University

11 How many three pointers did Nick Van Exel make in 1994–95?

A. 183

12 Which team did Shaquille O'Neal play with before joining the Lakers?

A. Orlando Magic

Key Words

All-Star: a mid-season game made up of the best-ranked players in the NBA. A player can be named an All-Star and then be sent to play in this game.

assists: a statistic that is attributed to up to two players of the scoring team who shoot, pass, or deflect the ball toward the scoring teammate

blocks: when a defensive player taps an offensive player's shot out of the air and stops it from getting to the basket

conference: an association of sports teams that play each other

franchise: a team that is a member of a professional sports league

free agent: a player who is not under contract and free to sign with any team he or she wishes

free throw: open or undefended shot at the basket taken from the foul line, also called foul shots

NBA Draft: the annual event in June where NBA teams select players from college to join the league. Teams select in order based on the prior season's winning percentages.

NBA Finals: the last round of the NBA Playoffs, where one team from the Western Conference plays another team from the Eastern Conference and the winner is crowned NBA Champion

playoffs: a series of games that occur after regular season play

rebounds: taking possession of the ball after missed shots

single-season record: a record set in a specific category for a franchise during an individual season

Index

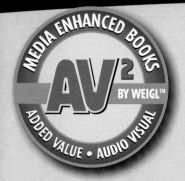

Log on to www.av2books.com

AV² by Weigl brings you media enhanced books that support active learning. Go to www.av2books.com, and enter the special code found on page 2 of this book. You will gain access to enriched and enhanced content that supplements and complements this book. Content includes video, audio, weblinks, quizzes, a slide show, and activities.

AV² Online Navigation

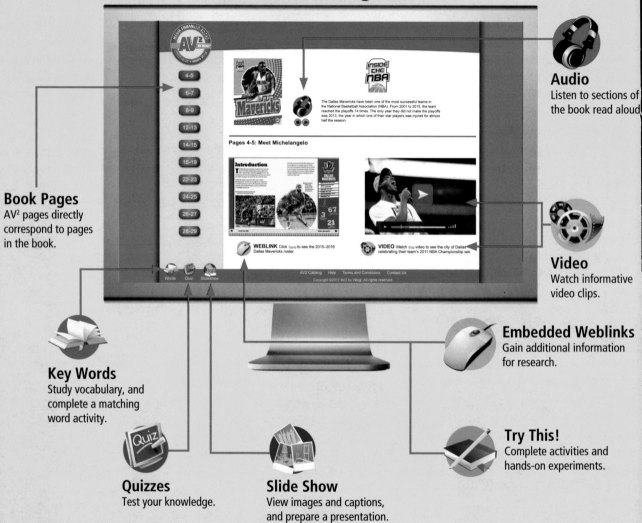

Audio
Listen to sections of the book read aloud.

Book Pages
AV² pages directly correspond to pages in the book.

Video
Watch informative video clips.

Key Words
Study vocabulary, and complete a matching word activity.

Embedded Weblinks
Gain additional information for research.

Try This!
Complete activities and hands-on experiments.

Quizzes
Test your knowledge.

Slide Show
View images and captions, and prepare a presentation.

AV² was built to bridge the gap between print and digital. We encourage you to tell us what you like and what you want to see in the future.

Sign up to be an AV² Ambassador at www.av2books.com/ambassador.

Due to the dynamic nature of the Internet, some of the URLs and activities provided as part of AV² by Weigl may have changed or ceased to exist. AV² by Weigl accepts no responsibility for any such changes. All media enhanced books are regularly monitored to update addresses and sites in a timely manner. Contact AV² by Weigl at 1-866-649-3445 or av2books@weigl.com with any questions, comments, or feedback.